THE BONE MARROW TRANSPLANT

BIOLOGY 4TH GRADE CHILDREN'S BIOLOGY BOOKS

Baby Professor

EDUCATION KIDS

HOW IMPORTANT IS BONE MARROW TO A HUMAN BODY?

Our body has 206 bones and in the center of many bones is a very essential substance that our bodies need. It's the bone marrow.

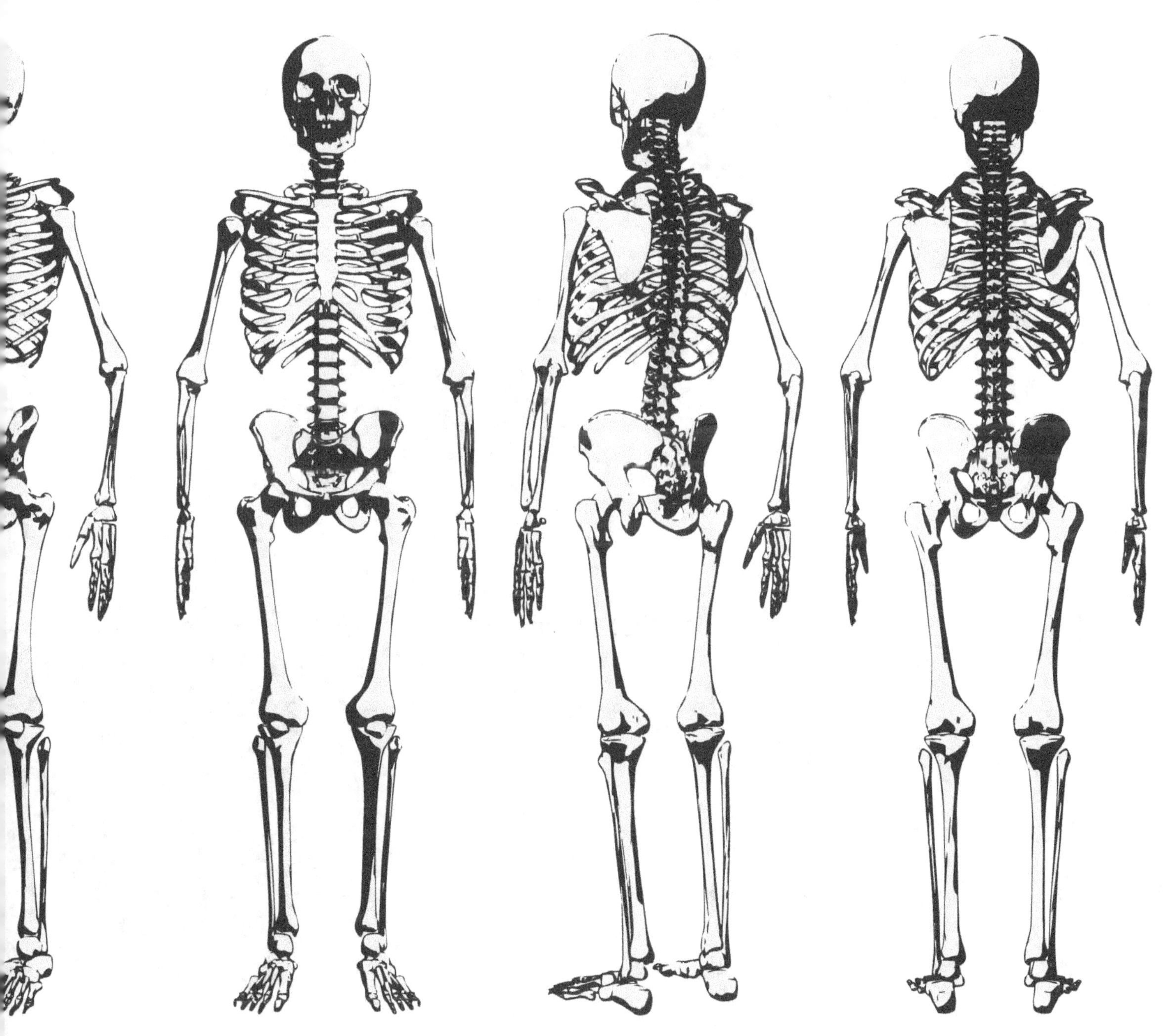

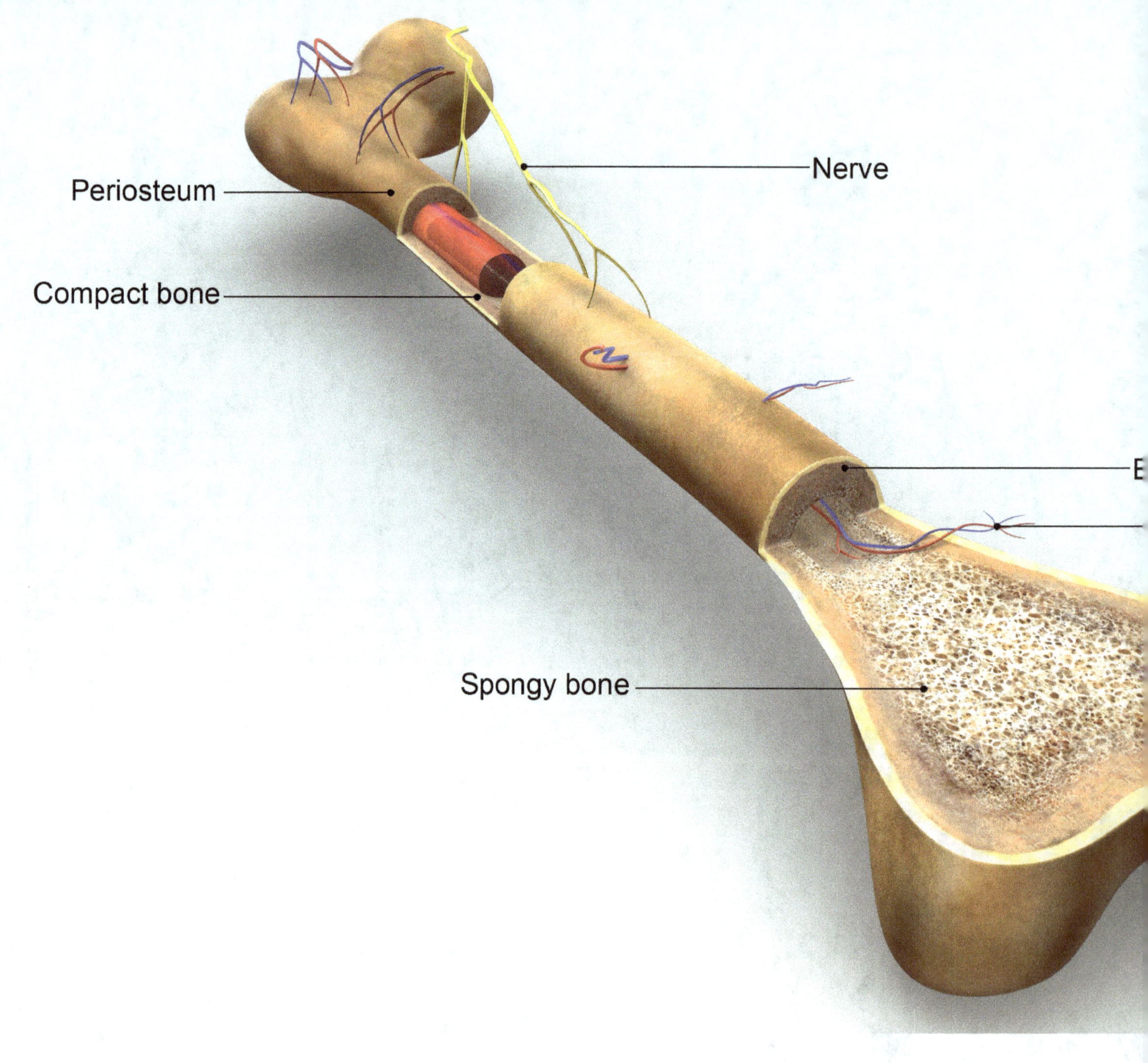

Nerve
Periosteum
Compact bone
Spongy bone

m

Blood vessels

Many of us don't know what bone marrow is. **Bone marrow** is a jelly-like substance inside our bones.

There are two types:

- red bone marrow
- yellow bone marrow.

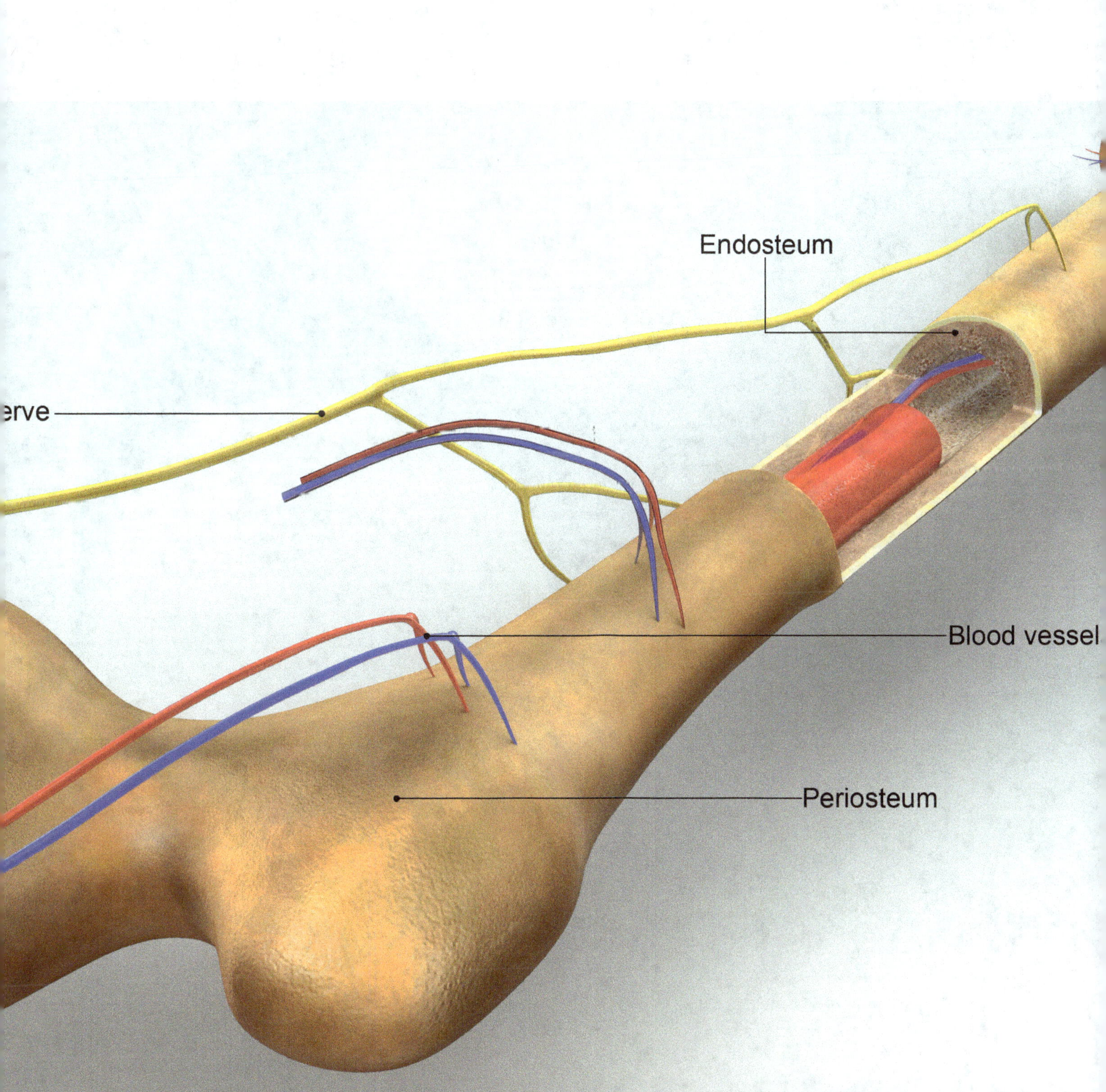

Endosteum
Nerve
Blood vessel
Periosteum

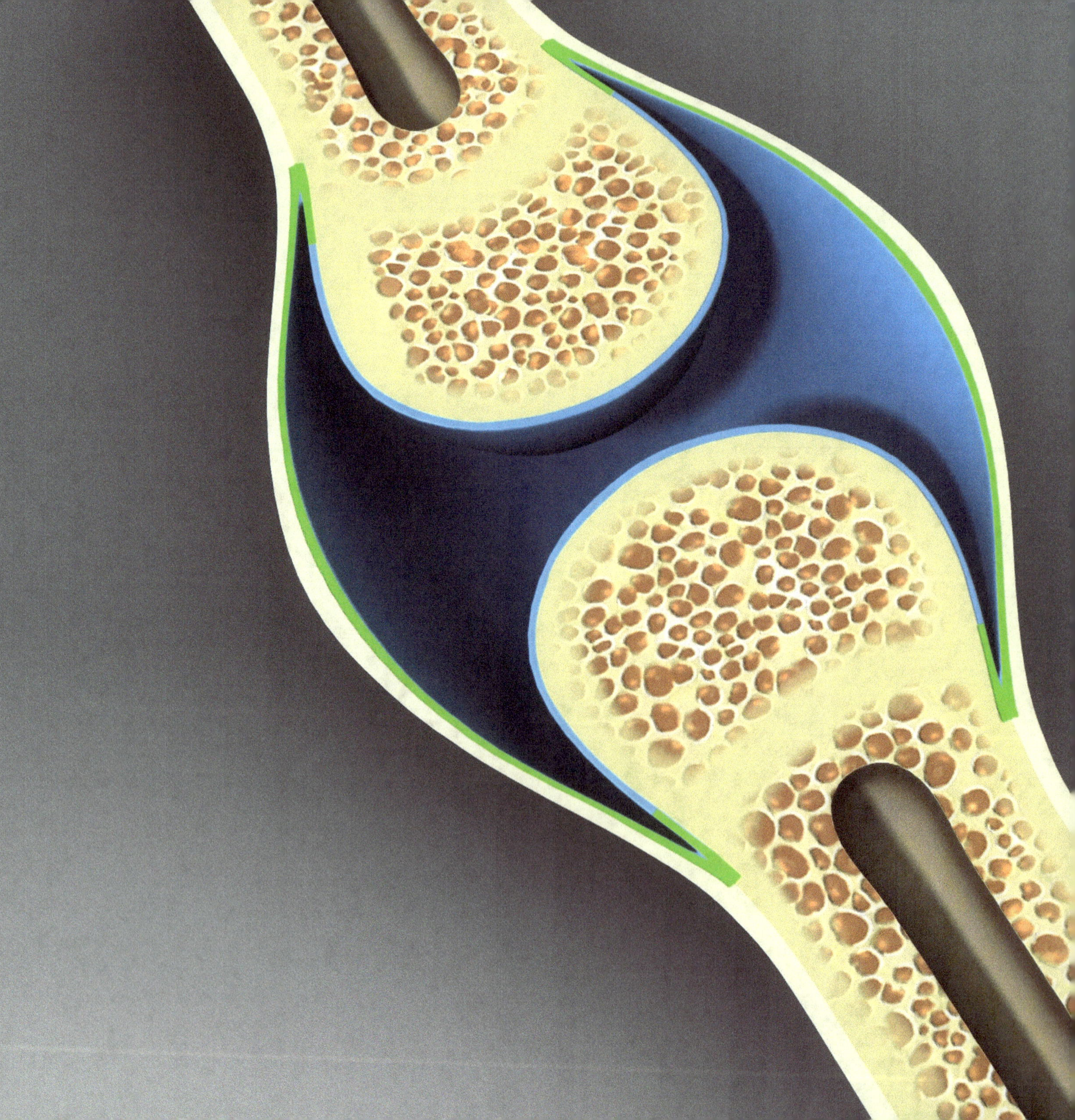

Yellow marrow is mostly made up of fat cells while **red marrow** produces red and white blood cells.

DO YOU KNOW THAT WHEN WE WERE BORN ALL OF OUR BONES HAVE RED MARROW?

But almost half of our bones will have red marrow when we become adults.

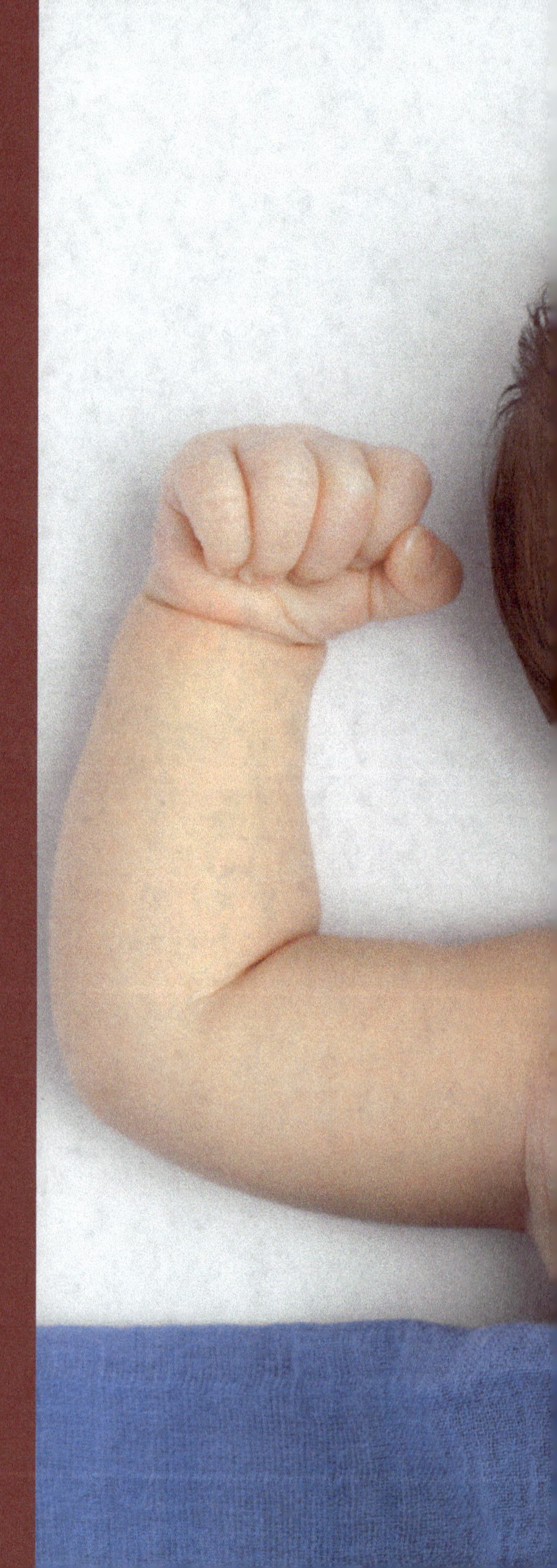

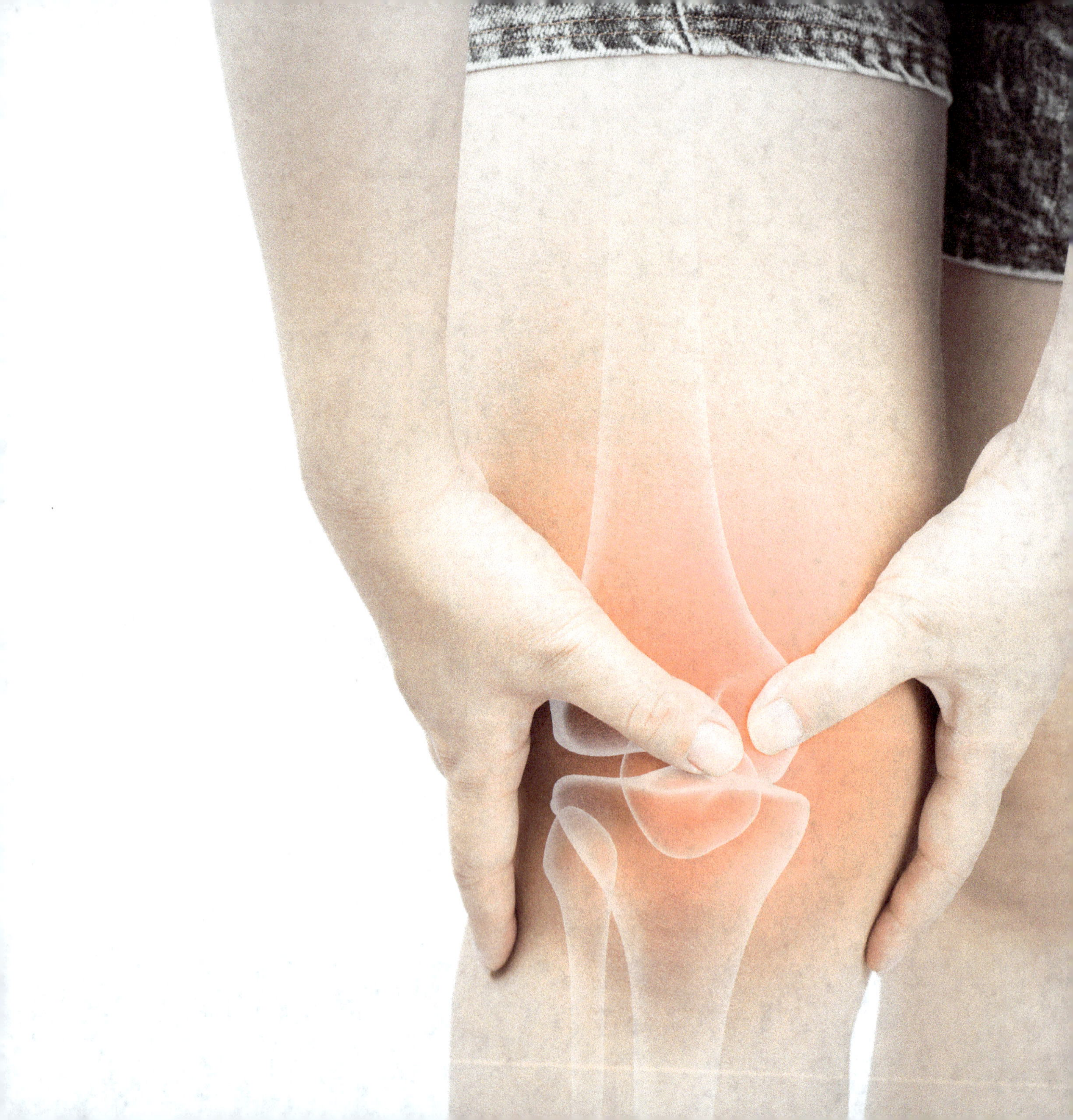

Now that we know what bone marrow is, it is high time that we learn the importance and function of bone marrow.

Our bone marrow helps
in the production of
platelets, red blood cells,
and white blood cells.

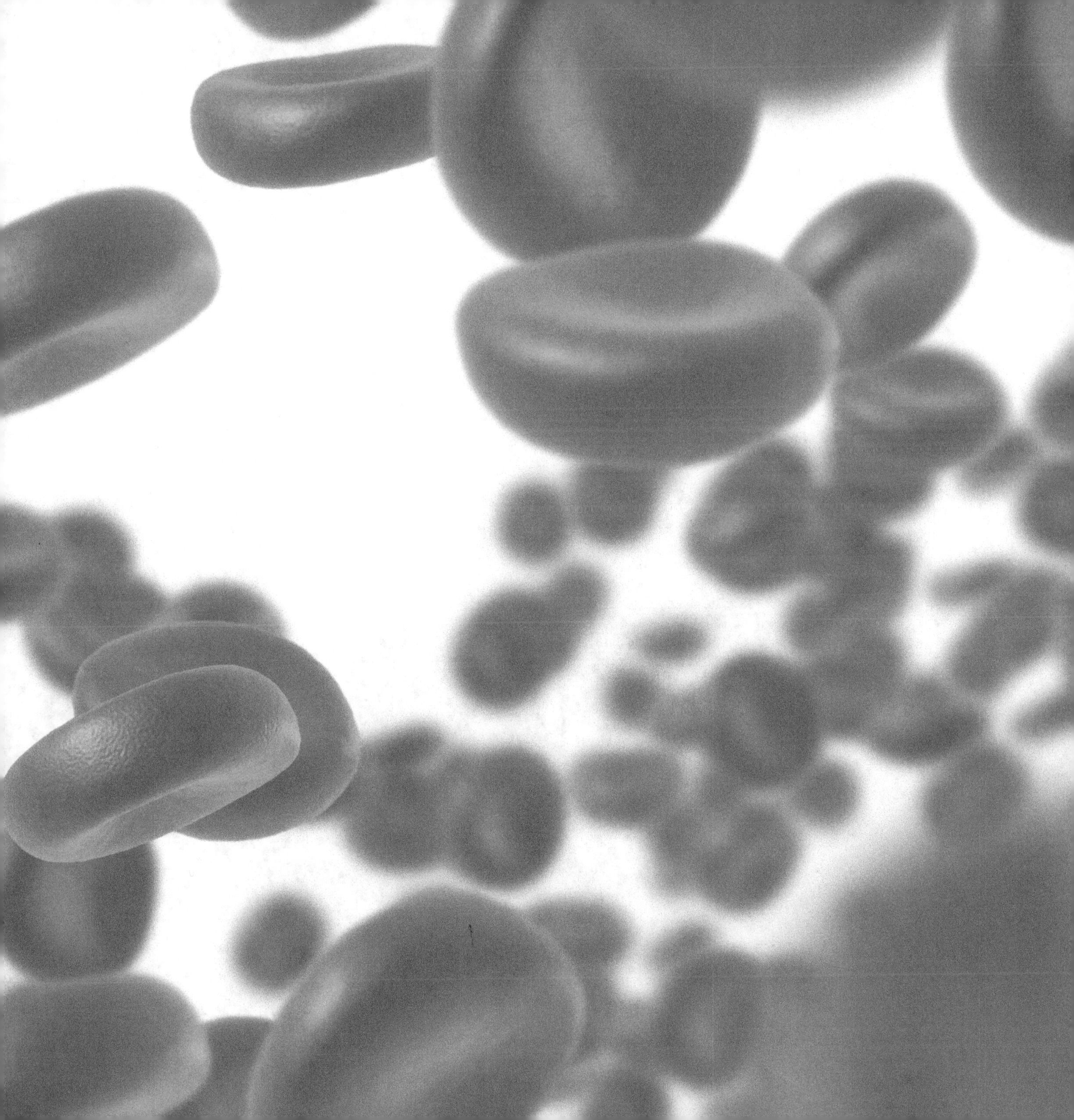

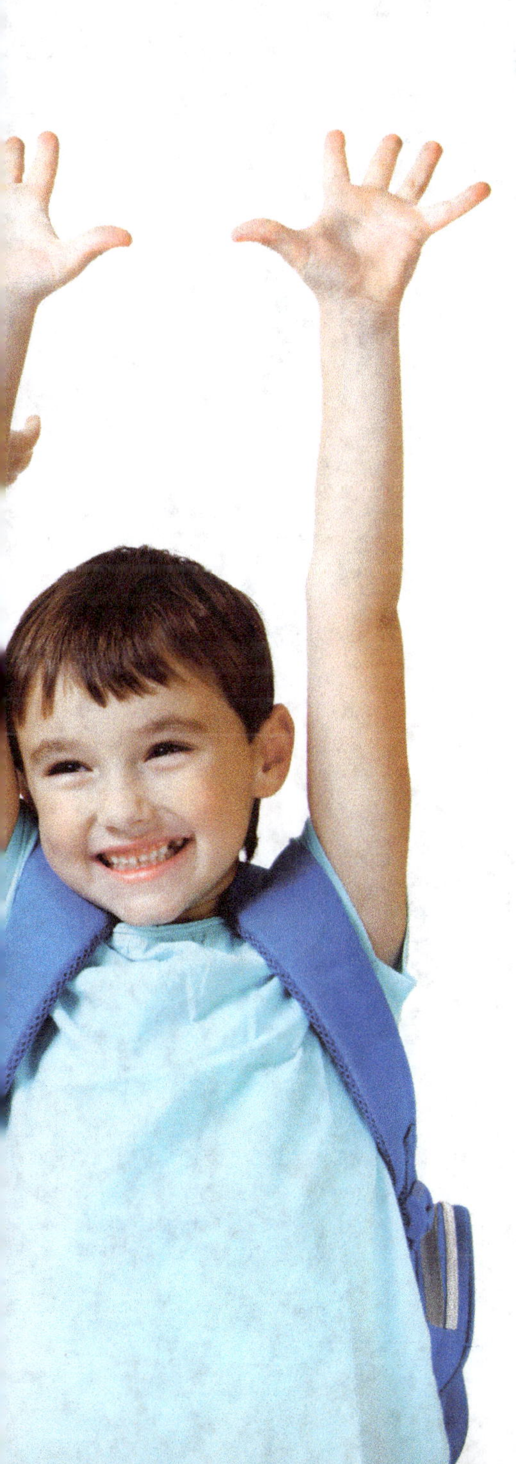

It can be found in different parts of our body, inside the bones of our skull, pelvis, spine, and shoulder blades.

Red blood cells transfer oxygen from our lungs to all parts of our body while white blood cells help fight infections and disease.

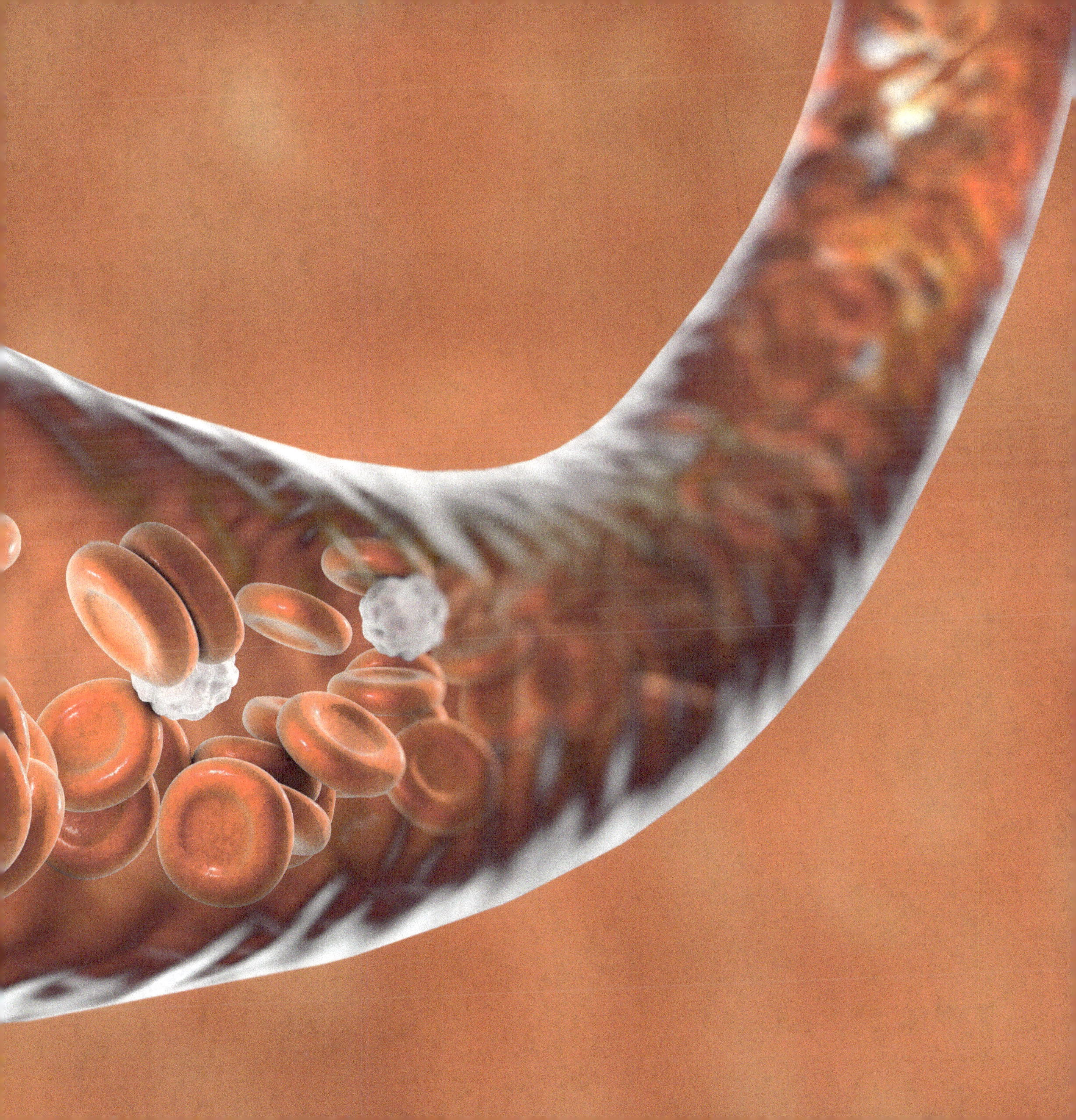

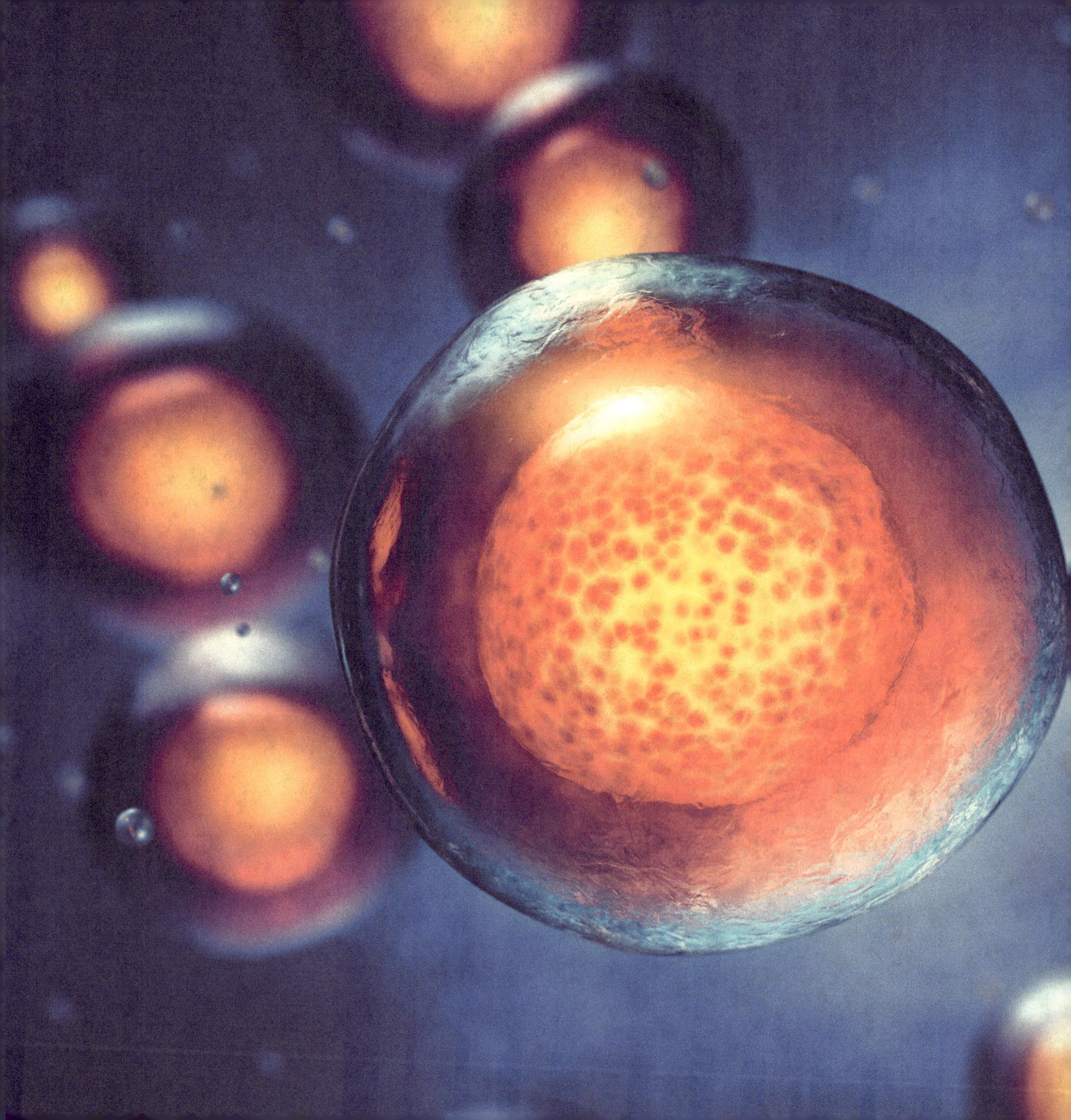

Platelets help in clotting the blood when you have a cut or injury.

BONE MARROW TRANSPLANT

What are some of the diseases that need bone marrow transplants?

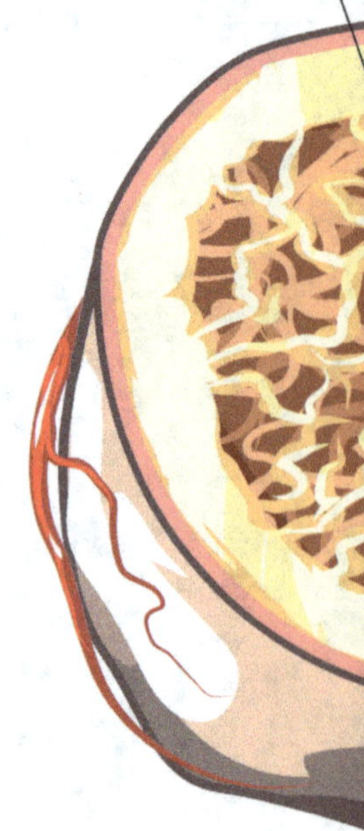

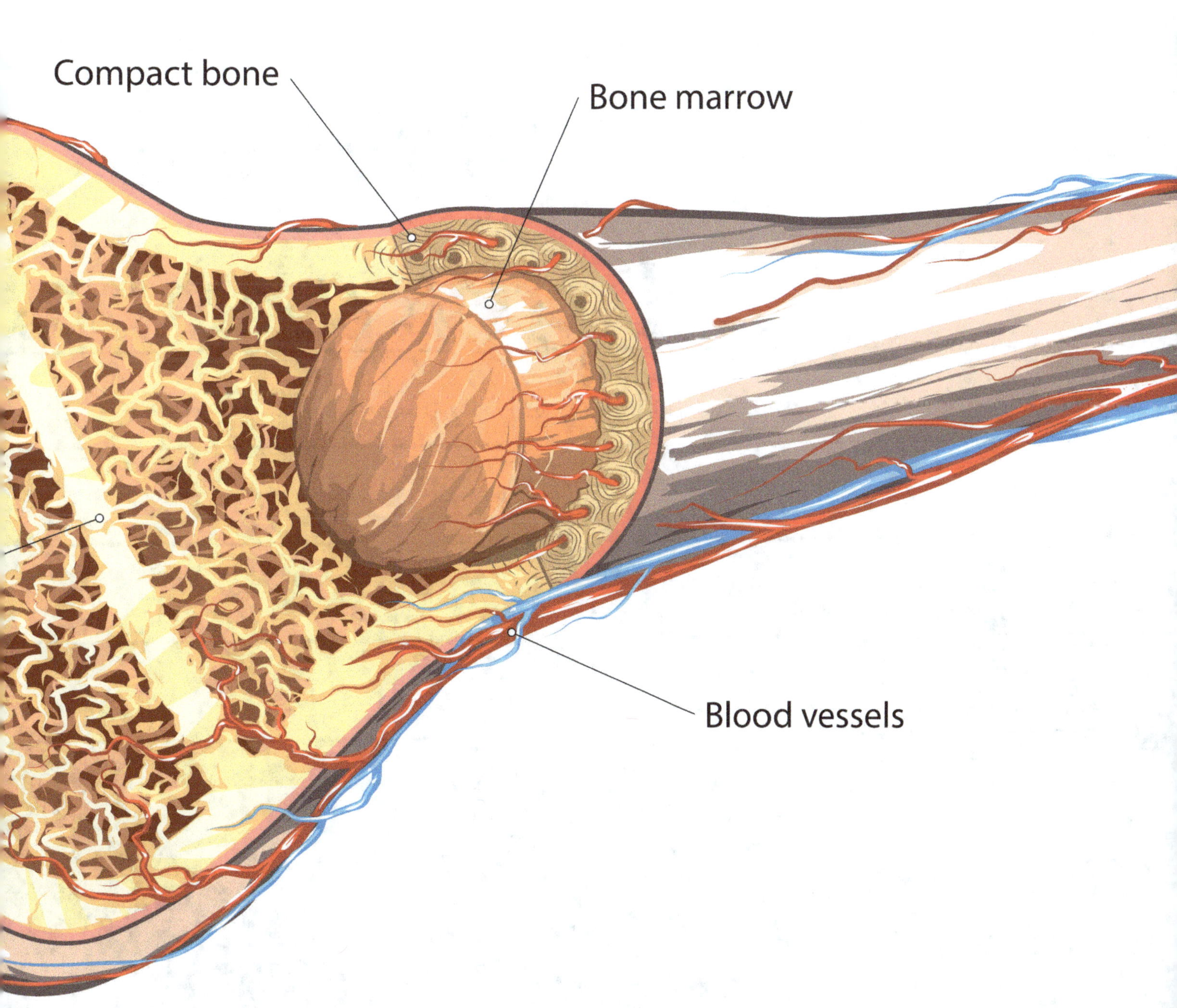

Compact bone
Bone marrow
Blood vessels

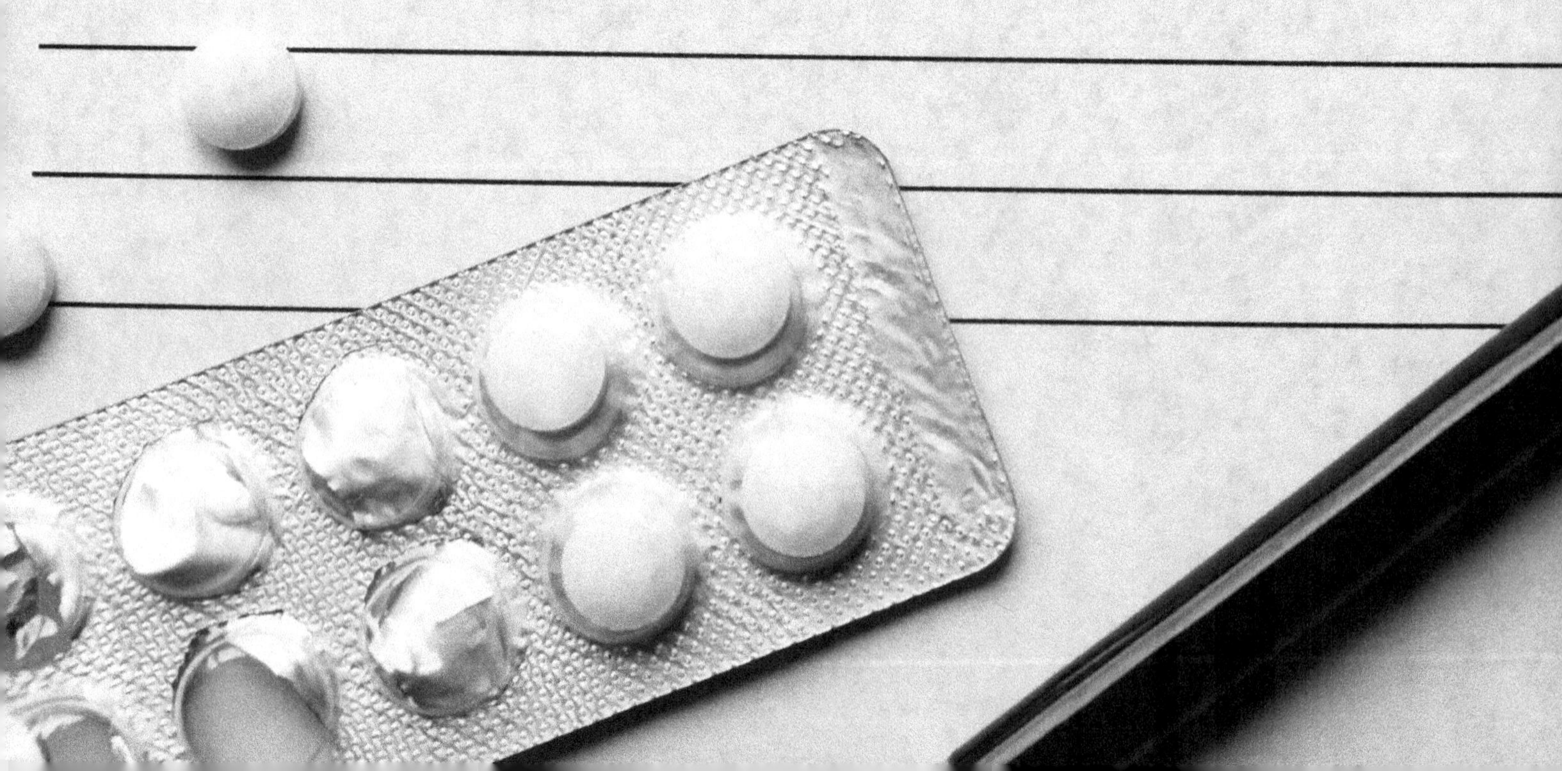

Height : _______________________
Weight : _______
Diagnosis
Lymphoma

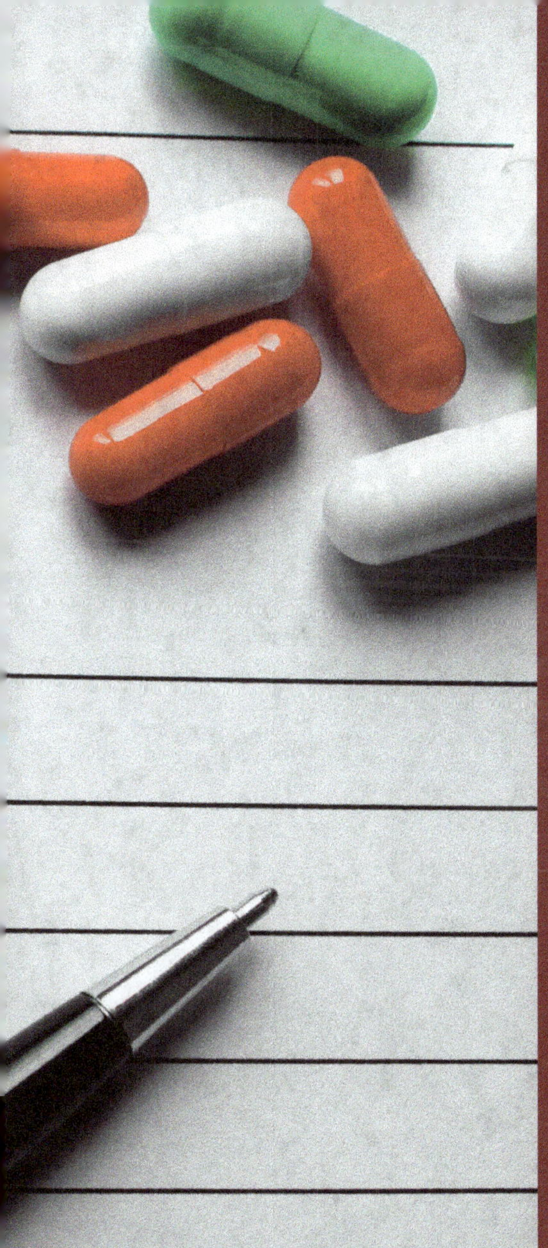

Some of the diseases are:

1. cancers like leukemia and lymphoma

2. aplastic anemia

3. damaged marrow due to chemotherapy

4. sickle cell anemia.

HOW DOES BONE MARROW TRANSPLANT WORK?

A bone marrow transplant is a medical process that replaces unhealthy bone marrow that has been damaged by a disease or infection with healthy bone marrow.

ONE
ARROW
NSPLANT

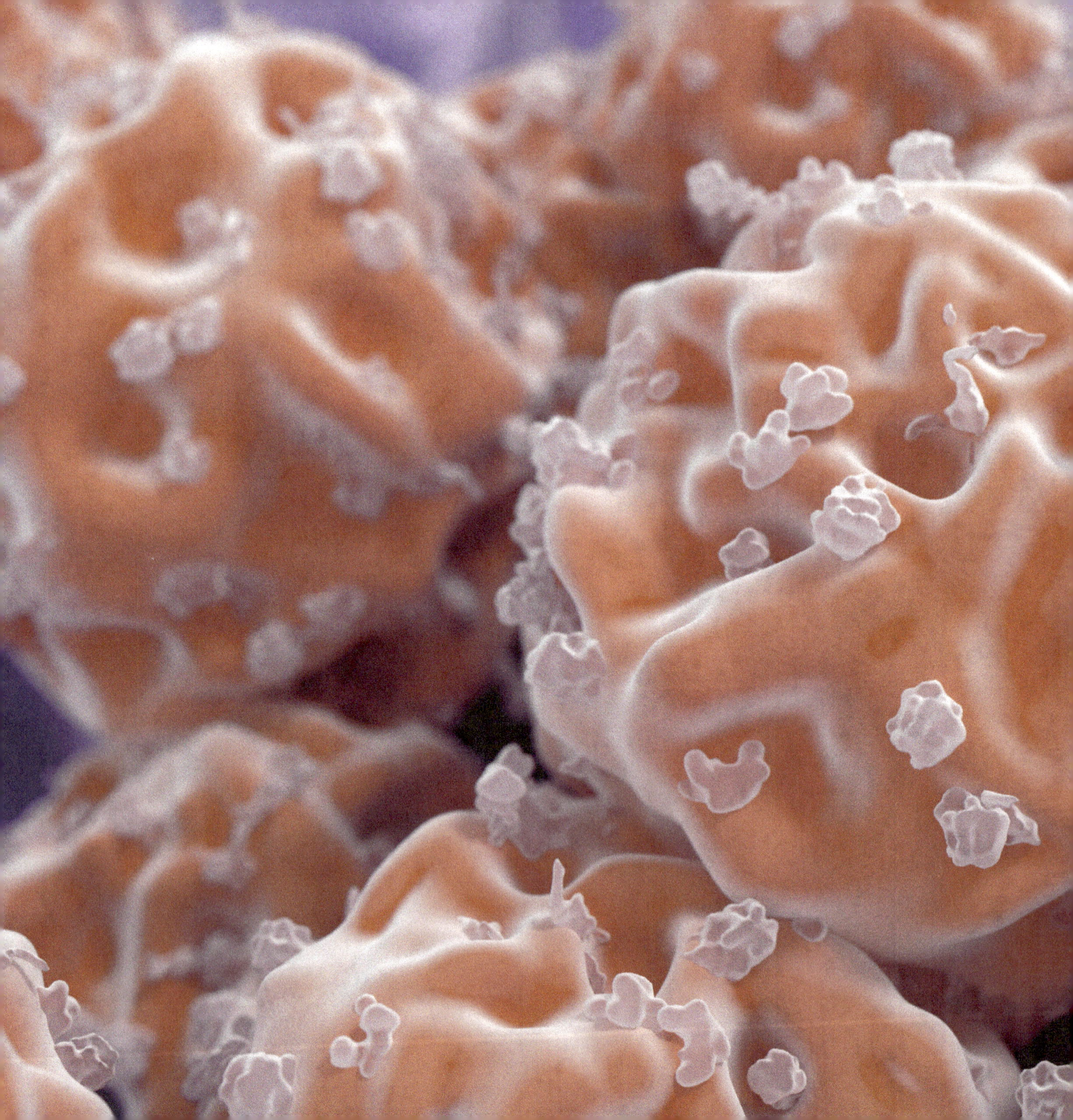

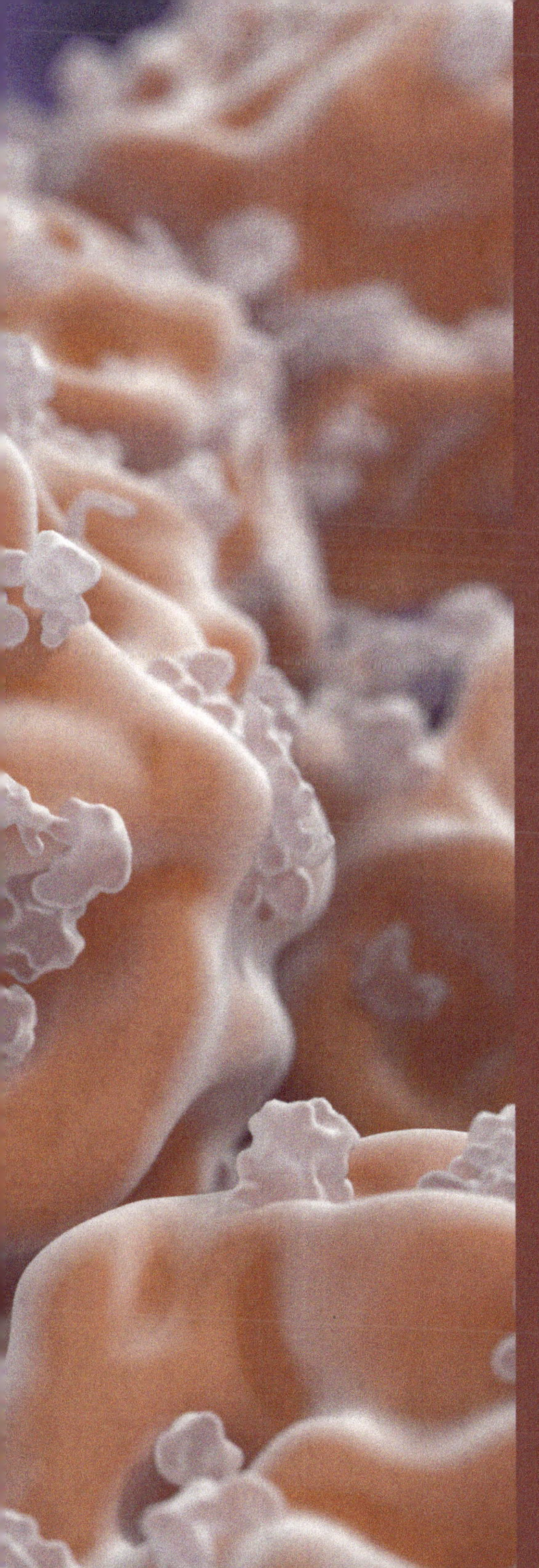

This transplant involves taking out stem cells from our bone marrow, filtering them, and then giving those stem cells back to either the patient where the cells were taken from or to another person.

Through this our body will then produce enough red blood cells, white blood cells, and platelets. It is very important that we keep our marrow healthy.

After a bone marrow transplant, a person may get complications such as headache, nausea, pain, chills, fever, shortness of breath, and a drop in blood pressure.

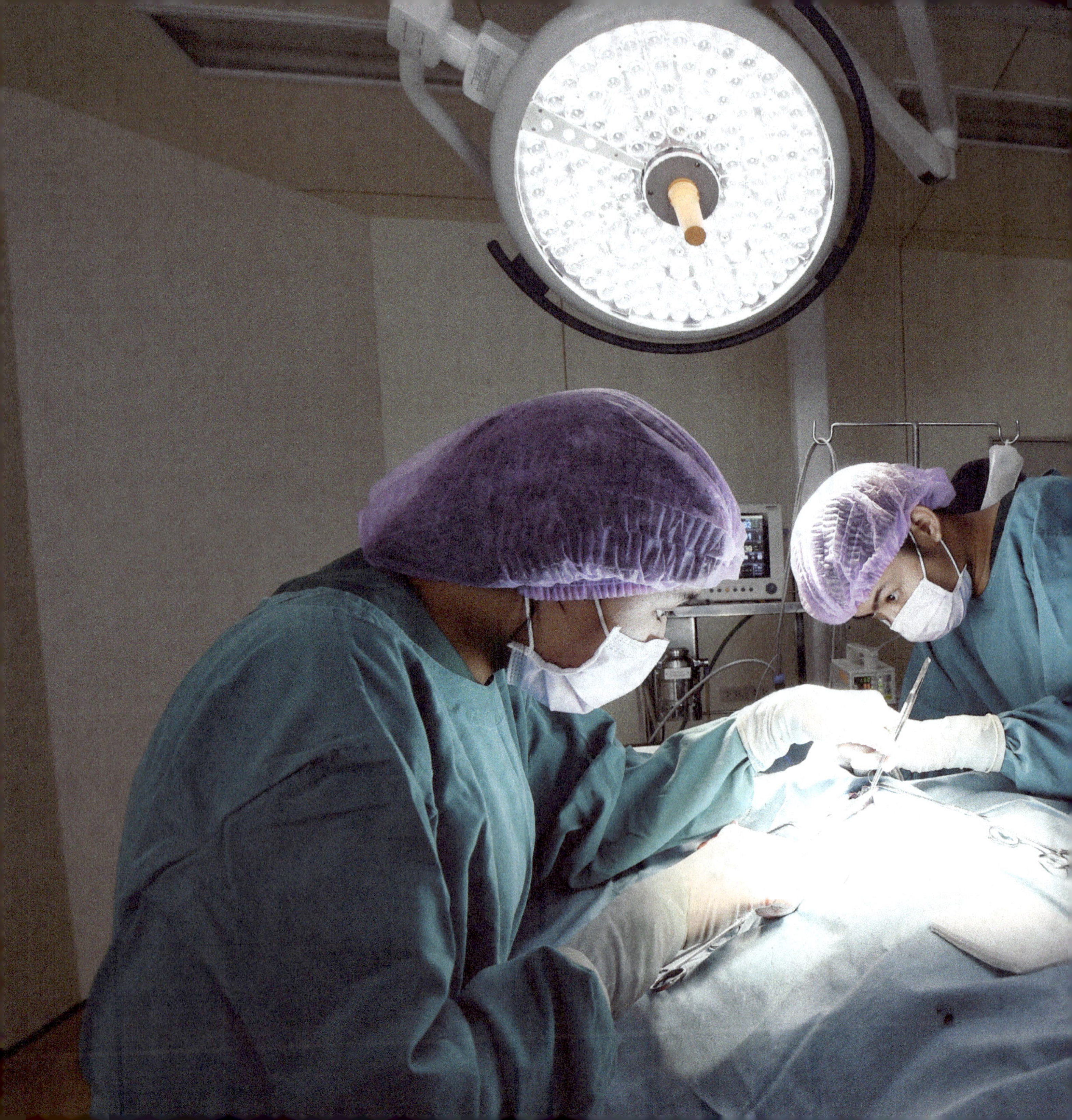

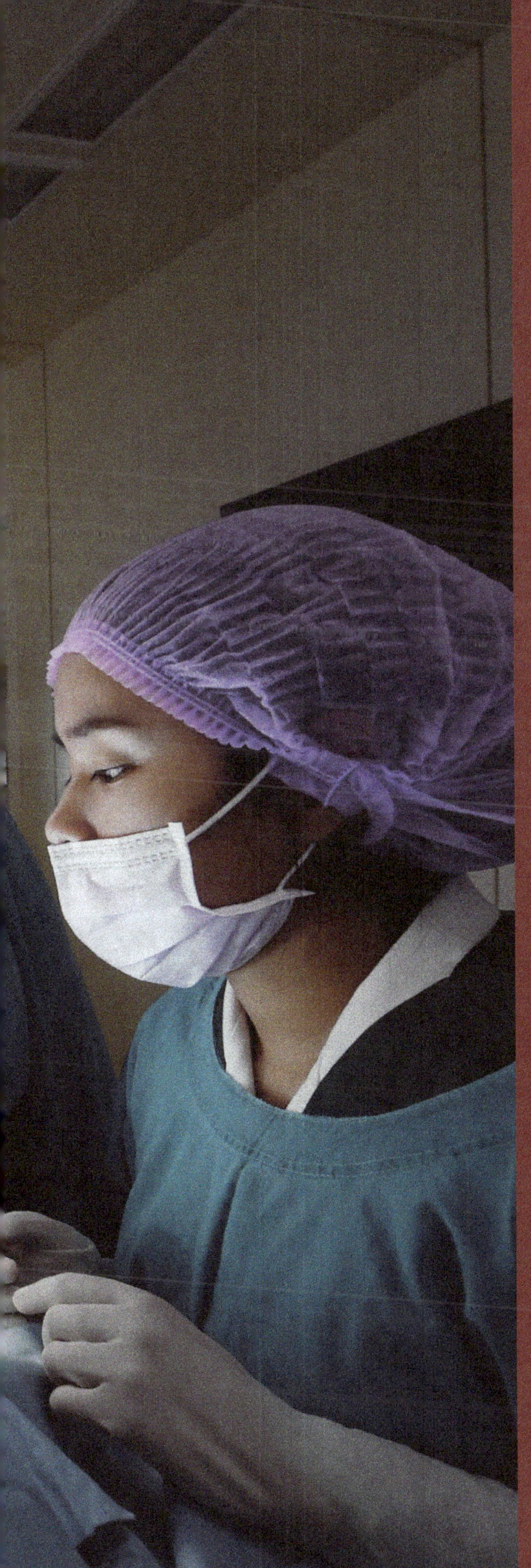

A bone marrow transplant can be risky to a patient since they may be on chemotherapy, radiation or even both before they undergo a transplant. This can be done in two ways through ablative treatment or mini transplant.

In an ablative treatment, a patient will undergo high-dose chemotherapy, radiation, or both to kill the cancer cells in the patient's bone marrow.

But here's the catch! It will kill the remaining healthy bone marrows but it gives way for the new stem cells to grow in the bone marrows, instead.

The mini transplant, on the other hand, also known as reduced intensity treatment is an exact opposite of the ablative treatment.

Before patients will undergo a transplant they will be given a lower dose of chemotherapy and radiation.

DO YOU KNOW THAT THERE ARE THREE TYPES OF BONE MARROW TRANSPLANT?

Yes! We may think that there is only one type of bone marrow transplant but fortunately specialists discovered different ways in treating bone marrow diseases.

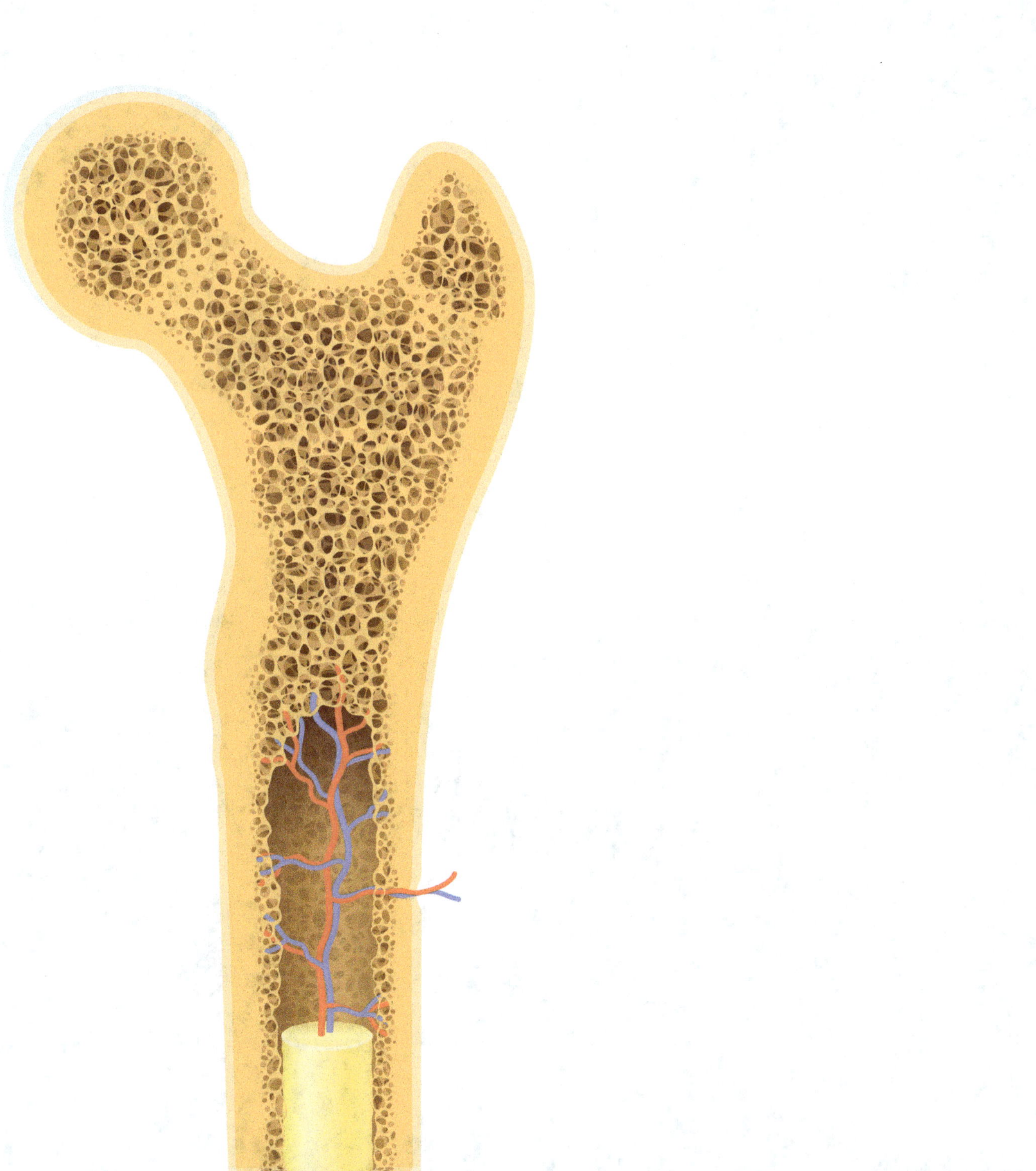

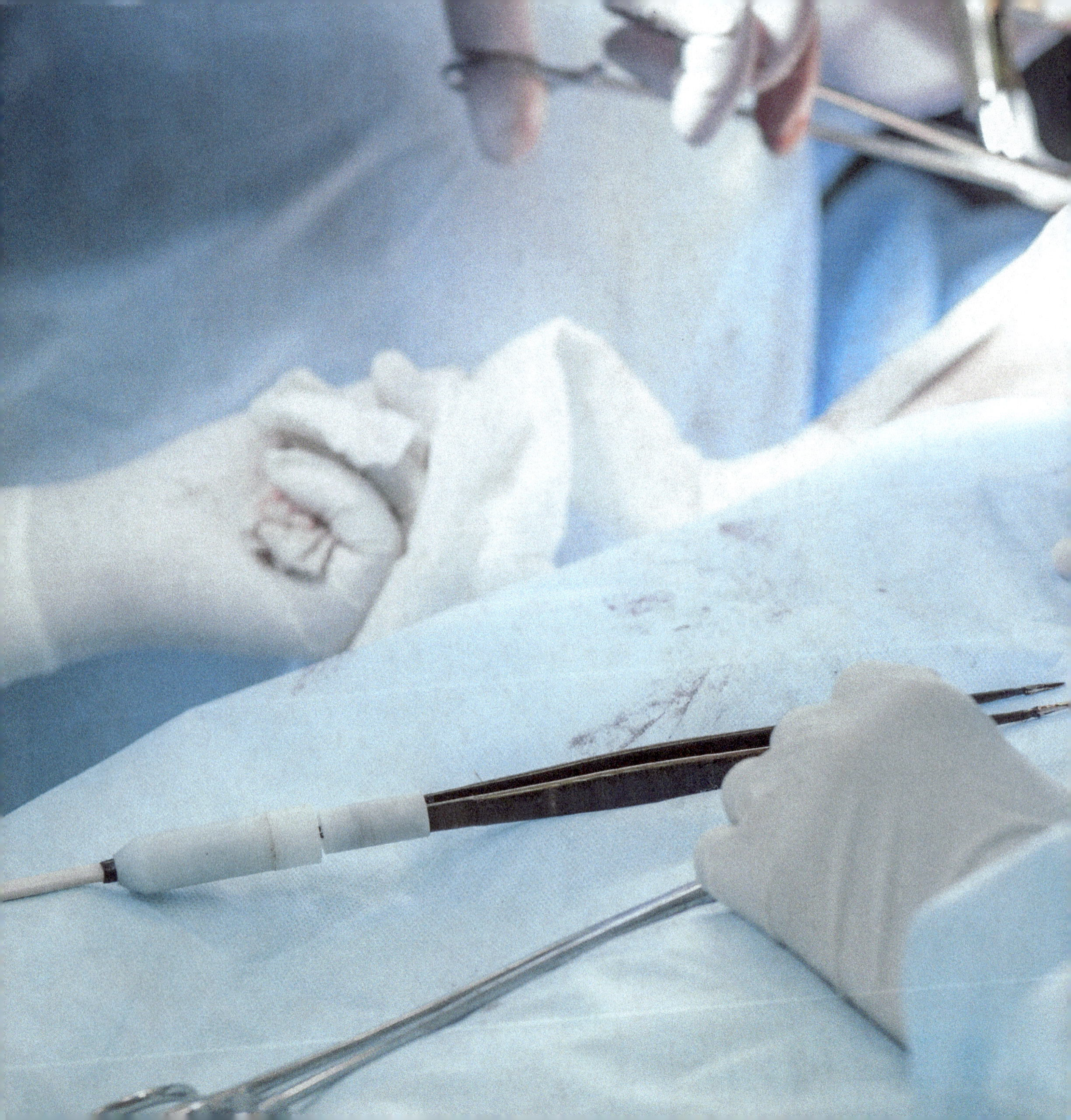

These are the Autologous bone marrow transplant, Allogeneic bone marrow transplant, and the Umbilical cord blood transplant.

An autologous bone marrow transplant is also known as rescue transplant. This procedure will remove the stem cells of a patient and store it in a freezer before they will be given a high-dose of radiation and chemotherapy.

Afterwards, the stem cells will then be put back to the patient's body thus making it as normal blood cells. Allogeneic bone marrow transplant is quite different from the autologous bone marrow transplant.

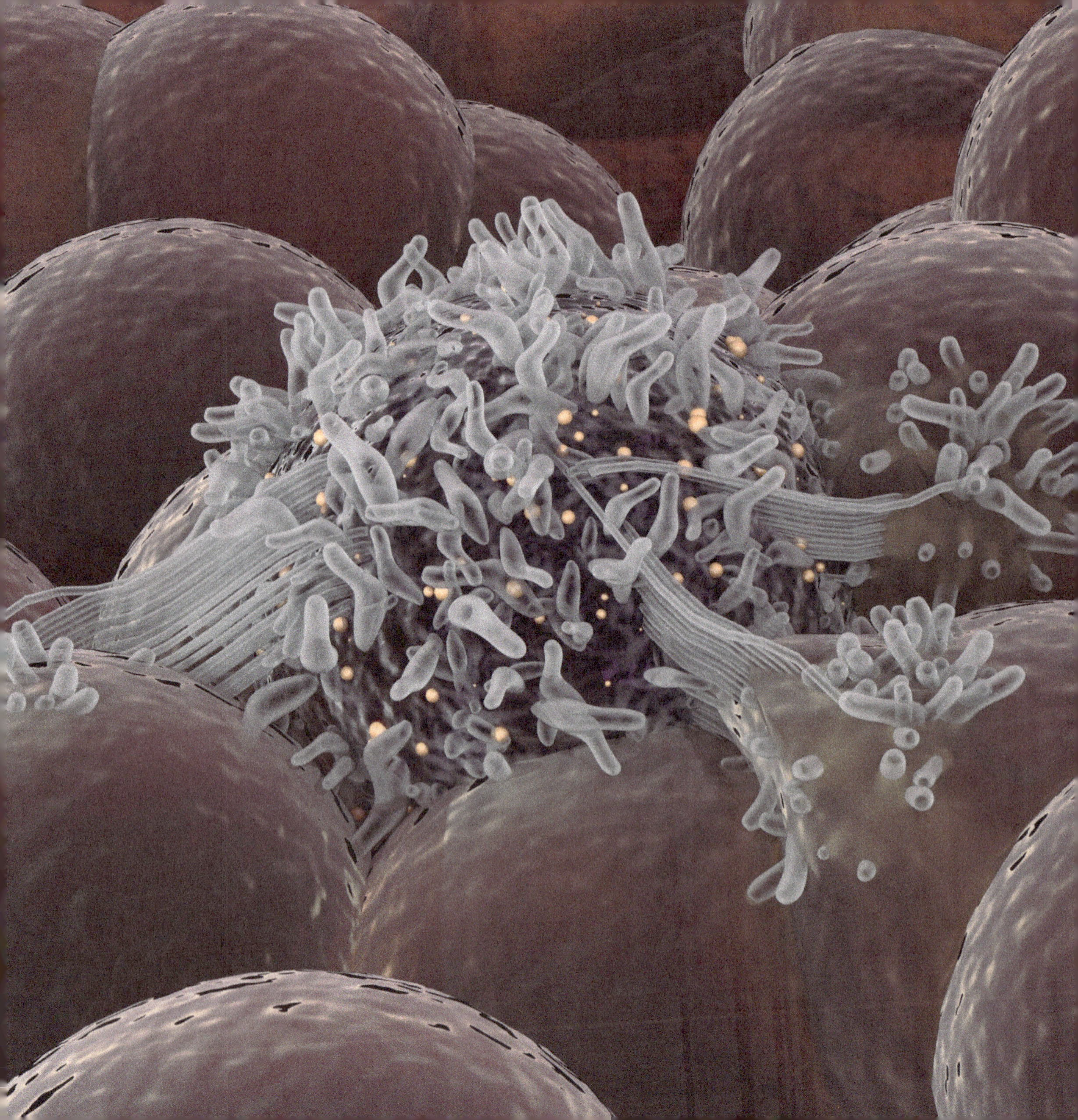

In this procedure, a patient needs to have a donor of the stem cells. Stem cells will be removed from the donor.

But before doing that, the donor will have to go through special tests to make sure that the donor is a good match for the patient.

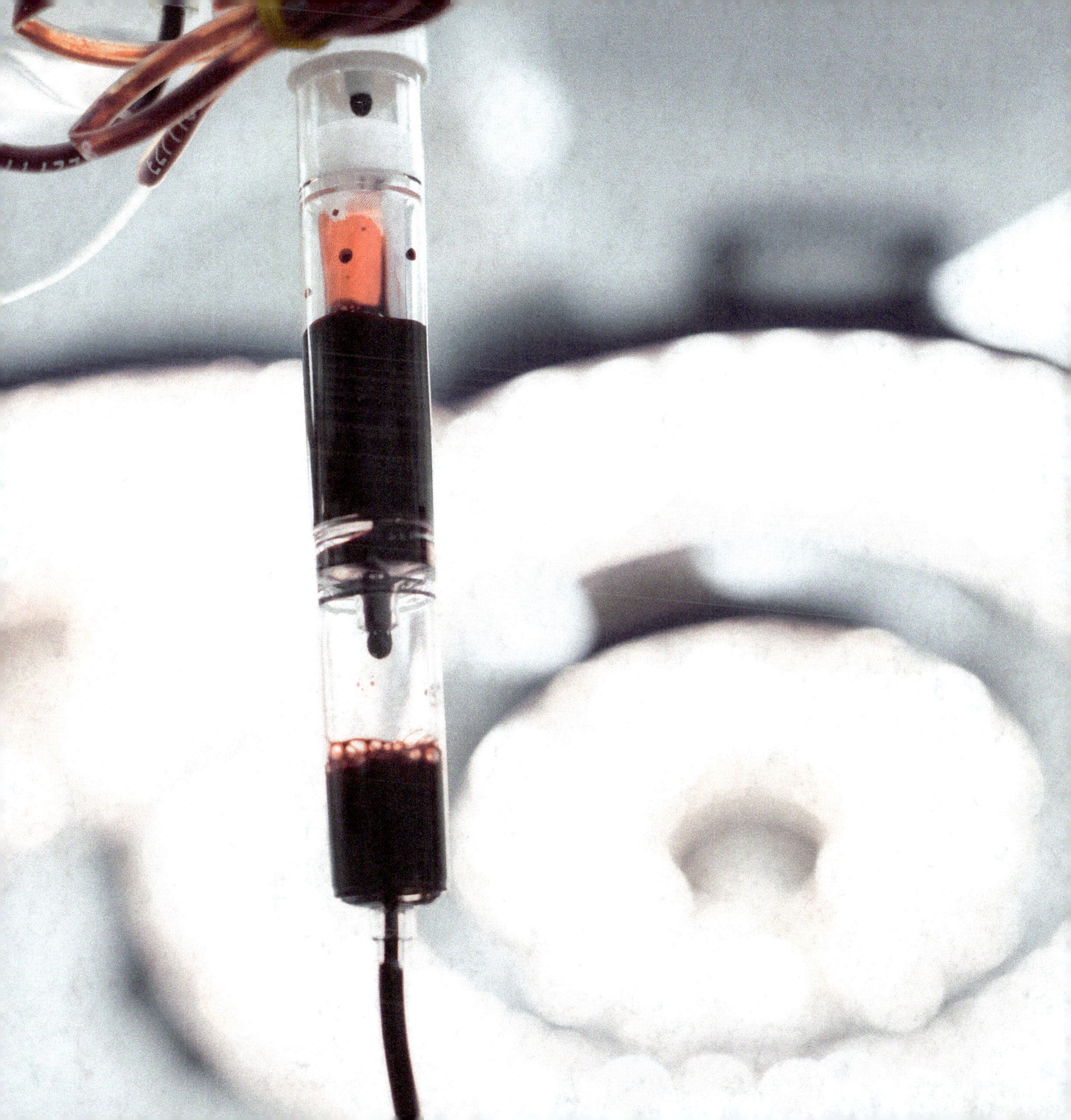

A good match will most likely be the patient's brother or sister. The patient's parents, child and even relatives can also sometimes be good matches.

Lastly, the umbilical cord blood transplant involves removing the stem cells in the umbilical cord of a newborn baby right after birth.

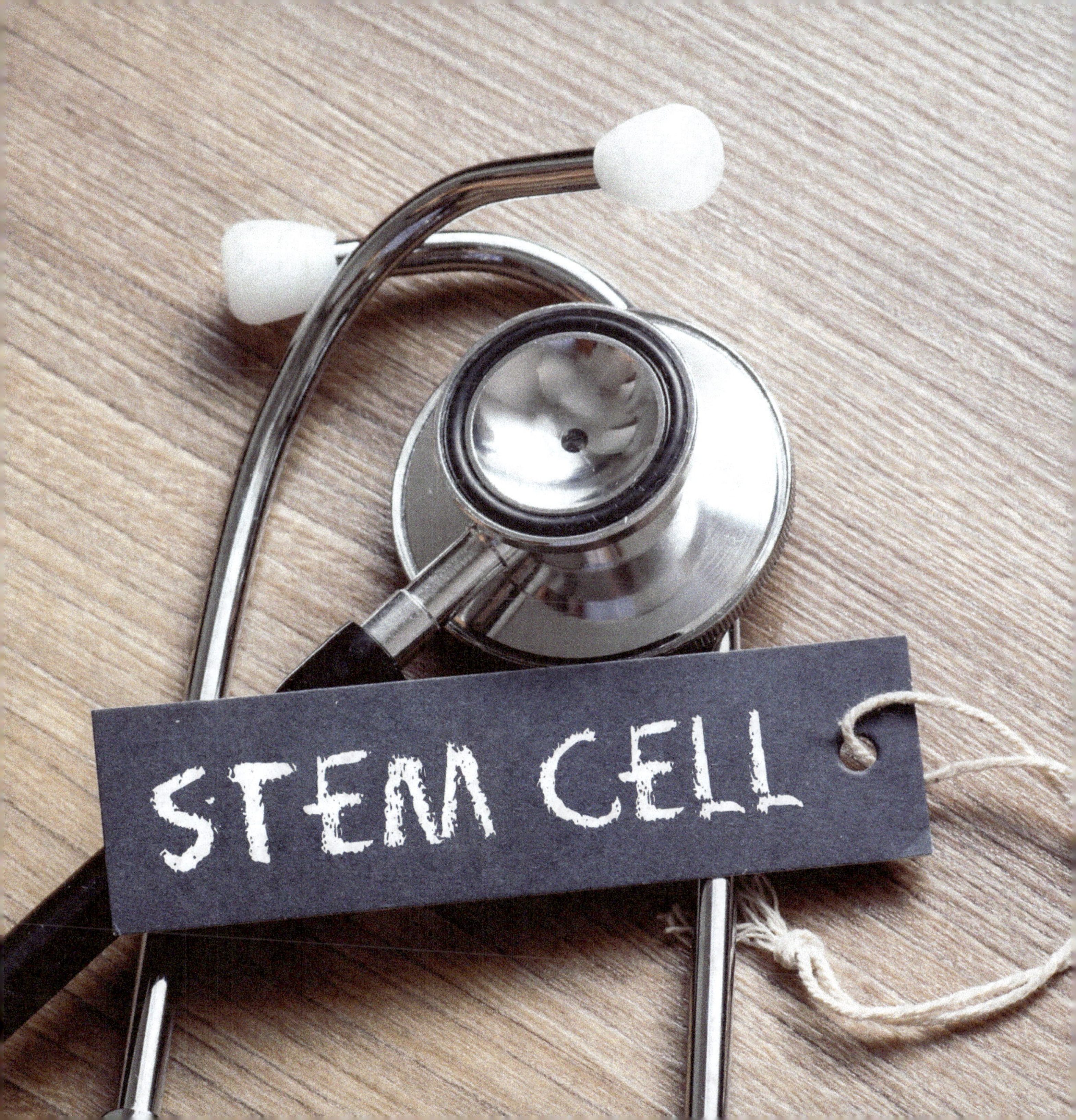
STEM CELL

The stem cells will then be stored into the freezer and will be used once the transplant happens.

The good thing about the blood cells in a newborn baby's umbilical cord is that they are still very immature so there won't be a problem of matching it with the patient's blood cells.

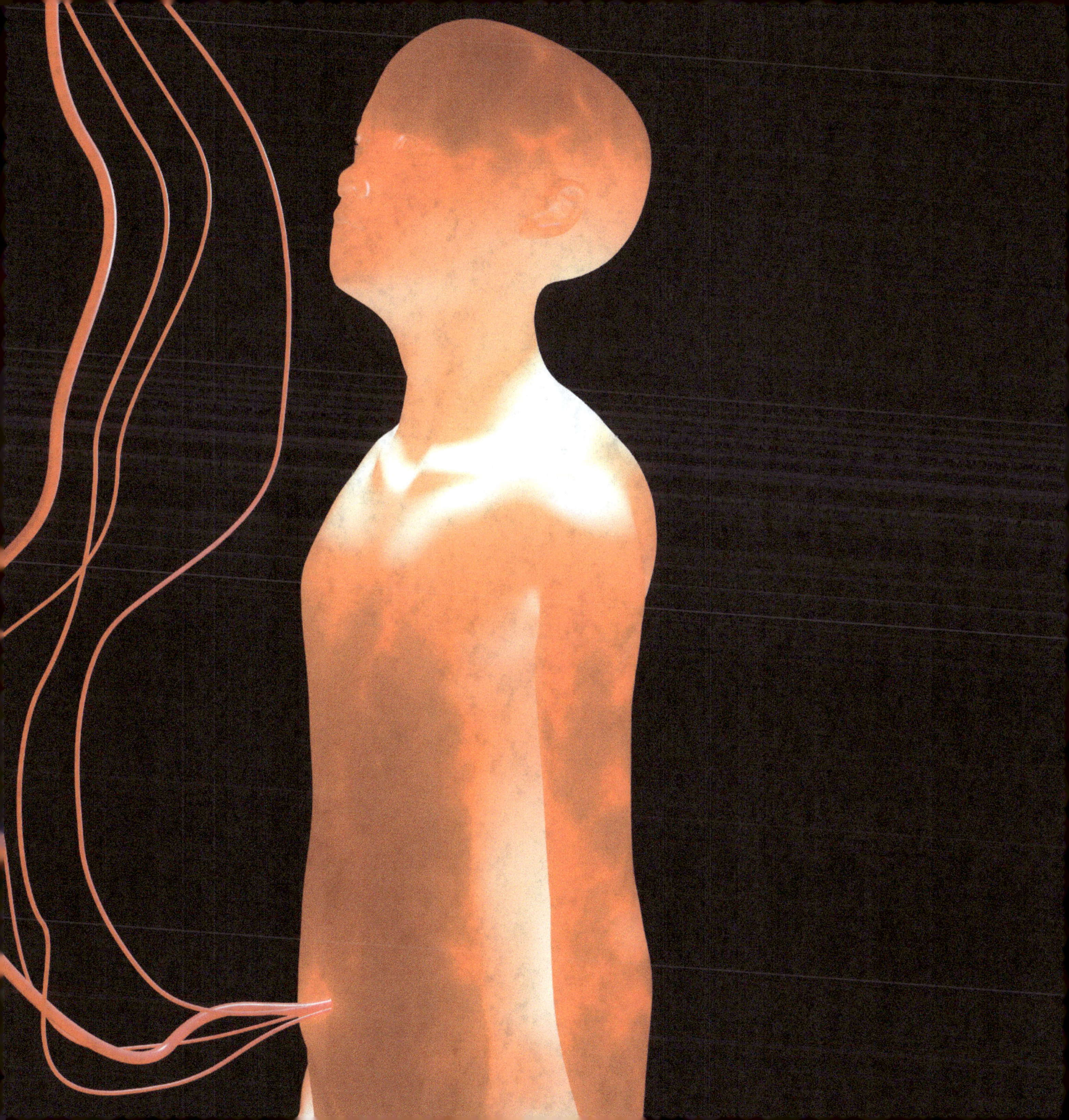

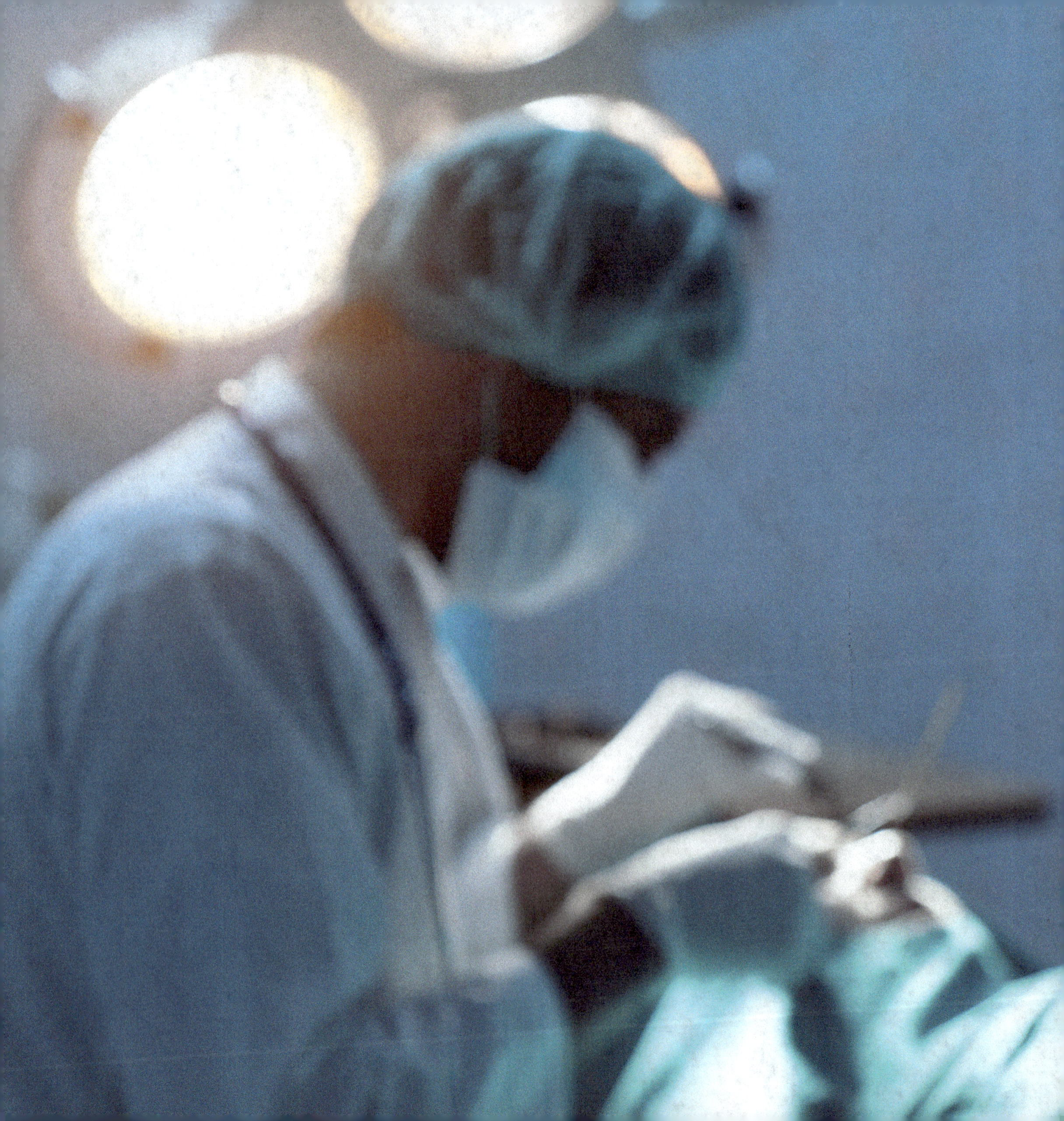

Any of those types of bone marrow transplants can effectively treat bone marrow diseases. A bone marrow transplant needs special care from doctors.

We need to take care of
our health so we will get
rid of different diseases.
Knowing about the bone
marrow keeps us aware of
its function in our body.

Visit

www.BabyProfessorBooks.com

to download Free Baby Professor eBooks
and view our catalog of new and exciting
Children's Books